As per NCF 2023

ECHOES

A Course in Listening and Speaking

Shefali Ray

Series Editor
K. Rajeevan

CLASS 4

OXFORD
UNIVERSITY PRESS

OXFORD
UNIVERSITY PRESS

Oxford University Press is a department of the University of Oxford. It furthers the University's objective of excellence in research, scholarship, and education by publishing worldwide. Oxford is a registered trade mark of Oxford University Press in the UK and in certain other countries.

Published in India by
Oxford University Press
22 Workspace, 2nd Floor, 1/22 Asaf Ali Road, New Delhi 110002, India

First Edition published in 2015
Second Edition published in 2025
Second impression 2025

ISBN-13: 9789361030543

Typeset in Poppins Regular
by Recto Graphics, Delhi 110096
Printed in India by Thomson Press India Ltd.

Illustrations by Weaverbird Interactive, New Delhi 110088
Cover design by Educatup Learning Pvt. Ltd.

Introduction

Welcome to ***Echoes: A Course in Listening and Speaking***, a competency-based, digital-rich, blended learning language lab that fits in your bag!

Echoes adopts an interactive approach to develop the communication skills of learners in a graded manner based on an international framework of learning and assessment. It includes tasks for preparing students for the Assessment of Listening and Speaking (ALS). This edition additionally incorporates the twin aims of the **National Curriculum Framework (NCF) 2023**—communicative competence and language proficiency. Further, *Echoes* helps accomplish **Curricular Goal 1 (CG-1) of Preparatory Stage set out in the NCF** which aims for learners to develop oral language skills using complex sentence structures to understand and communicate ideas coherently.

Course Objectives

The course aims to teach learners:

1. to pronounce English words accurately, laying stress on the right syllables
2. to lay stress on the correct words in a sentence depending on the meaning that is to be communicated
3. to speak fluently and appropriately in various real-life contexts using the correct intonation, proper pauses, and combining or omitting sounds as needed
4. to develop oral and aural skills by breaking-down grammatical forms and sentence structures, enabling granular learning with effective carry over
5. to become successful communicators through sustained practice in diverse authentic situations
6. to read aloud poems, dialogues and texts efficiently, and hold debates and discussions with the guidance and support provided

Key Features of the Course

Echoes deploys all types of activities listed in the **NCF 2023** under the strategies for Oral Language Development: picture conversations, sharing experiences, storytelling and role-play.

Learner-friendly visuals and layout.

Comic strips that introduce the topic and provide an enjoyable start to the learning process.

Use of real-life conversations in authentic situations.

Grammar-based explanations coupled with application-based activities.

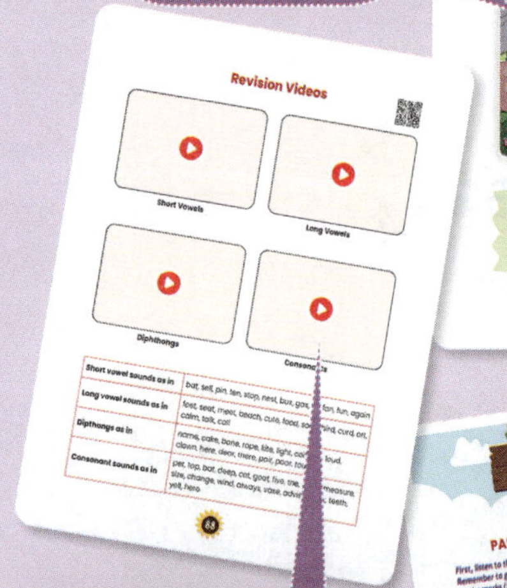

QR-code enabled access to digital resources such as audio and animation on **Oxford Educate***—the digital companion to *Echoes*.

Animation videos that show correct mouth movement for pronunciation at the end of each grade.

Dedicated read-aloud pages with pauses and stresses marked to show how speech works.

Each book has multiple structured and unstructured tasks along with audios that form a part of the listening and speaking activities. Use them as many times as needed to help learners familiarise themselves and learn the natural rhythm of the language.

*To access Oxford Educate, go to https://www.oxfordeducate.in

How to use *Echoes*

Each unit of *Echoes* has a relevant **communicative function** and **grammatical structure/ language expression** in focus. These are combined seamlessly with the listening and speaking activities that use everyday conversations to help learners become better at communication. *Echoes* is modelled in such a way that the twin aims of introducing a topic and providing regular practice are achieved through each and every task through the grades.

Here's a basic approach to using the book:

- Use the lead-in activity to introduce the communicative function in focus in the unit. You can play the animation either from **Oxford Educate (OE)** or by scanning the QR code for greater visual engagement. Have a discussion on the use of specific grammatical structures that are explained in the box at the end of the graphic story.
- To do the various activities, demonstrate one item as an example. Let learners listen to the audio files twice or even more, if necessary. They can access the files either directly from **Oxford Educate** or by scanning the QR codes.
- In the **listening** exercises, make learners listen to the audio files on **Oxford Educate** and repeat the words, phrases, sentences and the dialogues in chorus as a class, then in smaller groups, and finally, individually. They can also access the files by scanning the QR codes.
- For the **speaking** activities, always demonstrate how to do the task. Then engage learners in the activity as instructed.

Oxford Educate: Revolutionizing Learning with Digital Innovation

Welcome to Oxford Educate, your ultimate digital learning companion for school books! This user-friendly intuitive app is designed to enhance the learning experience for both students and teachers, offering high-quality captivating animations and audio narrations that help students understand the various nuances of speech.

♦ Audio ♦ Animation ♦ Phonic videos ♦ Answer keys and listening texts for teachers

To access Oxford Educate, go to https://www.oxfordeducate.in or scan

Teacher Support

Finally, there's robust classroom and pedagogical support through teacher manuals that provide model lesson plans for optimal learning effectiveness.

Detailed Contents

Chapter No.	Communicative function in focus	Grammatical structures/language expressions in focus	Listening: learning outcomes	Speaking: learning outcomes
1.	**Comparing Objects and People** • C 1.1: Converses fluently and meaningfully in different contexts • C 1.3: Makes oral presentations	The use of comparatives *The book on the left has a thicker cover.* *My tail is longer and prettier than yours.* *Real flowers are more beautiful than paper flowers.*	• understand the words used to make comparisons • listen to short conversations and write the correct answer • listen to and recognize stress patterns in two-syllable words • listen to compound nouns where the ending sound of the first word and the beginning sound of the second word is the same	• practise pronunciation of compound words/phrases where the ending sound of the first word and the beginning sound of the second word is the same • practise stress patterns in two-syllable words • ask and answer personal questions • compare two similar looking pictures
2.	**Talking about the Past** • C 1.1: Converses fluently and meaningfully in different contexts • C 1.2: Summarises core ideas from material read out in class • C 1.3: Makes oral presentations	The simple past *I watched a movie last night.* *He gave me a job.* *We ate the biscuits.* *The merchant reached a land overrun with rats.*	• understand how we talk about the past • listen for stress difference between compound nouns and noun phrases • identify stress in polysyllabic words • listen for stress emphasis in short questions, commands, formulaic expressions and other phrases • listen to a conversation and match people with their actions	• pronounce compound nouns and noun phrases with the correct stress • ask and answer questions • interact with a partner to ask and answer questions about the past • talk about some actions in the past using visual clues
3.	**Making Offers** • C 1.1: Converses fluently and meaningfully in different contexts • C 1.2: Summarises core ideas from material read out in class • C 1.3: Makes oral presentations	The use of *shall* and *Can* to make offers *Shall I find it for you?* *Can I get you some water?* *Yes, please. Thank you very much.* *No, thank you. I'm fine.* *No, not now.*	• understand how to offer help to different people • listen to contractions • learn to identify sentences that are left out in a conversation • listen to words with endings where no stress shift happens: -able, -al, -er, -ful, -hood, -ing, -ise, -ish, -less, -ly, -ment, -ness, -ship • listen to words with endings where shift happens on the penultimate syllable: -tion, -cian, -ic, -ical • select the right answer by listening to a person's description of something	• pronounce words with endings where shift in stress does not happen: -able, -al, -er, -ful, -hood, -ing, -ise, -ish, -less, --ly, -ment, -ness, -ship • pronounce words with endings where stress shift happens: -tion, -cian, -ic, -ical • interact with a partner and make and respond to offers • make suitable offers after reading a text

Chapter No.	Communicative function in focus	Grammatical structures/language expressions in focus	Listening: learning outcomes	Speaking: learning outcomes
4.	**Expressing Reason/ Result** • C 1.1: Converses fluently and meaningfully in different contexts • C 1.2: Summarises core ideas from material read out in class • C 1.3: Makes oral presentations	The use of *because* and *so* to express reason/result. *Why did you leave early?* *I left early because my grandparents were coming home.* *I had the project work to finish. So I did not come out to play.*	• understand how to express reasons • identify the form of the verb • listen to the pronunciation of the words ending in 's' or 'es' • learn the pronunciation and stress patterns of compound nouns, adjectives, verbs and adverbs • fill up details by listening to a conversation • learn to ask for reasons and express reasons or results	• pronounce compound words • interact with a partner to ask reasons and give answers
5.	**Talking about Ongoing Actions in the Past** • C 1.1: Converses fluently and meaningfully in different contexts from material read out in class • C 1.3: Makes oral presentations	The past continuous *What were you doing at three in the afternoon?* *I was sleeping.* *I was finishing my Science project.* *We were chatting in bed when the earthquake struck.*	• understand how to talk about actions of the past • identify the actions of people from a passage • understand the different forms of 'ed' ending verbs and identify the last sound heard (/t/, /d/ or /id/) • listening to a monologue/ description of a place and filling in the missing details	• pronounce past tenses: /t/, /d/ and /id/ in isolation and in connected speech • say correct statements based on the description heard • ask and answer questions on ongoing actions at a certain time in the past
6.	**Expressing Possibility** • C 1.1: Converses fluently and meaningfully in different contexts • C 1.2: Summarises core ideas from material read out in class • C 1.3: Makes oral presentations	The use of *may* *I may go to my grandparents in summer.* *She may be at the toy stall.* *I may go out today.* *We may not go for a picnic.*	• understand how to express different possibilities • listen and mark the intonation of the words in bold • fill missing words after listening to a conversation • listen to sentences expressing possibility	• use different intonation for old and new information • express options in sentences using the right intonation • understand different warning signs and say what might happen if they are ignored • ask and answer questions on what one is likely to do in the next year
7.	**Talking about Actions in Relation to Other Actions** • C 1.1: Converses fluently and meaningfully in different contexts • C 1.2: Summarises core ideas from material read out in class • C 1.3: Makes oral presentations	The use of *before* and *after* *I left home before I had my breakfast.* *I was a happy jackal before I came to the village.* *You came after I did.* *She met me after I spoke to the teacher.*	• understand how one action is discussed in relation to another • complete a form after listening for specific information • listen to sentences about simultaneous actions in the past • understand the use of rising and falling intonation in different contexts • listen to a story with the correct intonation	• practise sentences expressing simultaneous actions in the past using appropriate intonation • practise phrases, clauses and a paragraph using rising and falling intonation • tell a story using the correct intonation

Chapter No.	Communicative function in focus	Grammatical structures/language expressions in focus	Listening: learning outcomes	Speaking: learning outcomes
8.	**Expressing Conditions** • C 1.1: Converses fluently and meaningfully in different contexts • C 1.2: Summarises core ideas from material read out in class • C 1.3: Makes oral presentations	Type I conditional clauses *If we light a fire in our camp we can keep animals away.* *If you go out, you will get wet.* *If someone sneezes in front of you, you should touch his/her head.*	• understand how to express conditions • match conditions with results • understand the use of intonation in dialogues • complete conversations by filling in the blanks	• say dialogues using rise and fall in the intonation • practise being a responsive listener by asking appropriate questions for more information or using expressions for follow up • complete an imaginary dialogue with a friend creatively and humorously and practise it with a partner
9.	**Making Suggestions** • C 1.1: Converses fluently and meaningfully in different contexts • C 1.2: Summarises core ideas from material read out in class • C 1.3: Makes oral presentations	The use of *Lets's* and *How about* *Let's switch off the AC and save some electricity.* *How about walking to school today?*	• understand how to make suggestions • fill details by listening for information • understand the use of stress in short conversations • identify the suggestions made by different people	• stress important words in conversations • practise short conversations by stressing the words in bold • use the rise and fall tones in short dialogues • play roles with a partner agreeing or disagreeing with the suggestions made • solve problems by understanding the situation and giving suggestions
10.	**Expressing Obligation** • C 1.1: Converses fluently and meaningfully in different contexts from material read out in class • C 1.3: Makes oral presentations	The use of *must* *You must eat your food on time.* *You must not answer any telephone calls from strangers.*	• understand how to express obligations • listen to a conversation and identify correct and incorrect sentences • listen and repeat sentences expressing obligation • understand the use of intonation in short conversations • mark the main words in a conversation that are said with emphasis or stress • fill in the missing details in a monologue	• stress important words in conversations • say sentences that express obligation • practise short conversations using rise and fall in intonation • complete sentences using must or mustn't according to the situation given and practise the same with a partner
	Read Aloud • C 1.3: Makes oral presentations		• listen to the passage and identify pauses, stress and intonation • listen to the audio and understand how to recite a poem	• read the passage aloud using the correct pronunciation, pauses, stress and intonation • recite a poem using the correct pronunciation, pauses, stress and intonation

Contents

Acknowledgements

© Alexandra Lande/Shutterstock (Taj Mahal, page 18); © Caron Badkin/Shutterstock (Taj Mahal, page 18); © David Evison/Shutterstock (Tiger Hill, page 44); © Rudra Narayan Mitra/Shutterstock (Darjeeling Toy Train, page 46); © Belokoni Dmitri/ Shutterstock (Dragonfruit, page 51); © Oxford University Press (Cow and calf, page 51); © Efired/Shutterstock (Safdarjung's Tomb, page 59); © Karunesh Johri/ Shutterstock (Qutub Minar, page 59); © CJM Grafx/Shutterstock (World's largest basket, page 80)

1 Comparing Objects and People

LISTEN AND LEARN

Listen to the conversation between the bear and the fox and notice how comparisons are made.

To compare two objects or people, we use the comparative degree of adjectives.

Adjective + **er** + **than...**

His handwriting is neater than mine.

Note: Some adjectives change their forms completely, like **good—better**, **bad—worse**, etc.

To compare something or someone with many, we say:

Adjective + **er** + **than everyone else's/Adjective** + **est**

Her work is better (good) than everyone else's.

Of the three apples, this one is the sweetest (sweet).

LISTEN AND MARK

Listen and encircle the correct option.

1. Where will Sunita spend a few days with her brother?

A

B

C

2. Which bus will she take?

A

B

C

3. What will the weather be like in Uttarakhand?

A

B

C

4. How far did he have to go for the medicine?

A

B

C

5. Which place will he go for dinner?

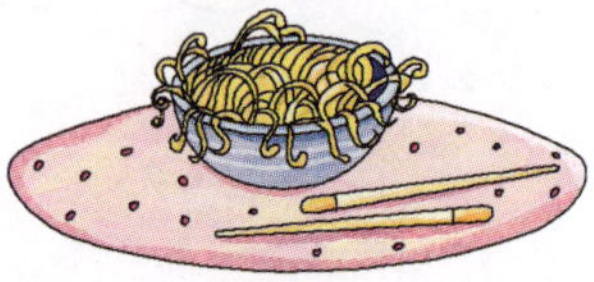

A

B

C

LISTEN AND WRITE

Listen and fill in the right words.

Location: Disneyland is in California and Magic Kingdom is in ....

Features: Both have the same kind of buildings and rides.

Size: Magic Kingdom is .... than Disneyland.

Buildings: Buildings at Magic Kingdom are .... than those at Disneyland. But the ones at Disneyland are ....

Streets and distances: The streets at .... are wider and the distance from one building to another is .... than that in Disneyland.

Wait-time: Wait-time in the lines is longer at ....

Rides: Rides at Disneyland are ....

Remember to use '**more** +adjective' while using adjectives that have more than one syllable, like **more beautiful**, **more honest**, **more interesting**.

LISTEN AND LEARN

Look at the pictures. Listen and repeat.

1. The blue shoe is newer than the green one.

2. Real flowers are more beautiful than paper flowers.

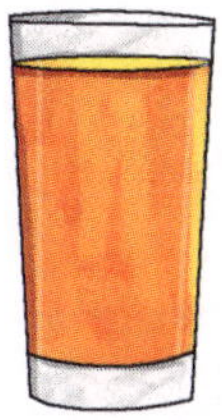

3. Coconut water is more refreshing than a soft drink.

4. Robin's dog is friendlier than Peter's dog.

5. The book on the left has a thicker cover.

SPEAK RIGHT

Listen and repeat.

1. bad day
2. book case
3. same match
4. nice socks
5. part time
6. tough fellow
7. next time
8. white tie
9. look carefully
10. line number
11. past tense
12. maximum marks
13. chewing gum
14. lamp post
15. black cat
16. car race
17. team mate
18. web browser
19. trunk call
20. traffic cone

Often, two nouns or an adjective and a noun are put together and treated as one word/idea. These are called **compound nouns**. In compound nouns, when the ending sound of the first word and the beginning sound of the following word is the same, one of them is dropped and the two words are said together as one word.

LEARN SOUNDS

Listen and repeat.

1. Stress the first syllable in bold in these nouns.

apple	**ar**tist	**bal**cony	**ber**ry	**bi**cycle	**cap**tain
chimney	**don**key	**dri**ver	**edi**tor	**fab**ric	**far**mer
helmet	**gro**cer	**jig**saw	**le**tter	**lio**ness	**liz**ard
medal	**mon**key	**nap**kin	**na**tion	**on**ion	**ra**dio

2. Stress the first syllable in bold in these adjectives.

angry	**aw**ful	**bro**ken	**cap**tive	**emp**ty	**fa**mous
friendly	**glo**bal	**hap**py	**hun**gry	**jea**lous	**joy**ous
lucky	**mo**dern	**nas**ty	**naugh**ty	**play**ful	**pret**ty
stupid	**shab**by	**thirs**ty	**tra**gic	**va**cant	**wool**ly

3. Stress the second syllable in bold in these verbs.

es**cape**	be**gin**	be**lieve**	col**lect**	com**pare**	de**cide**
dis**card**	en**quire**	per**mit**	ex**plore**	for**get**	in**spire**
main**tain**	mis**take**	nar**rate**	pre**pare**	pro**tect**	re**ceive**
re**quest**	re**move**	re**ward**	sub**mit**	suc**ceed**	u**nite**

LISTEN AND MARK

Listen and underline the syllable that is stressed in the given words.

1. anxious
2. dragon
3. discover
4. enjoy
5. follow
6. funny
7. gossip
8. lovely
9. manage
10. master
11. plenty
12. table
13. tiger
14. wagon
15. whisper

Many nouns and adjectives having two syllables, like **collar**, take the stress on the first syllable.

Many verbs having two syllables, like **enjoy**, take the stress on the second syllable.

ROLE-PLAY

Ask and answer.

Talk to a partner and seek information about the following.

1. What's your name? My name is ....
2. Which state are you from? ....
3. How many members are there in your family? ....
4. What food do you like the most? ....
5. When do you wake up every morning?
   At/At about/Before ....
6. When is your birthday? On ....

READ AND SPEAK

Look at the two pictures. Compare them. Read the sentences and complete them. Take turns to say the sentences.

A

B

1. Which picture is brighter?

   I feel .... is brighter.

2. In which picture is the Taj Mahal closer?

   The Taj Mahal seems closer in ....

3. In which picture does the Taj Mahal look whiter?

   It looks ....

4. In which picture does the grass look greener?

   The grass looks ....

5. At what time was *Picture A* taken?

   I think it was taken in the ....

6. At what time was *Picture B* taken?

   I think it was taken at/in the ....

2 Talking about the Past

LISTEN AND LEARN

Listen to the story of Dick Whittington and notice how we talk about the past.

To talk about past events, use the simple past tense of verbs. The past tense of many verbs is formed by adding **'ed'** to the base form, like **walk—walked**, **pick—picked**.

In some verbs, instead of adding **'ed'**, their form is changed, like **hear—heard**, **make—made**, **is—was**, **begin—began**, etc.

LISTEN AND MATCH

Listen to a conversation. Who will do what? Select and match the activities with the names. Write the letter next to the names.

Beena ☐

Venkat ☐

A draw posters

B mime

C play the guitar

D teach hill songs to the music group

E prepare the western dance

F sing Gideon's songs

G write the dialogues

Gideon ☐

Manjeet ☐

Ira ☐

SPEAK RIGHT

1 *Stress the first word in these compound nouns.*

airport	**book**shop	**bus** stop	**chop**sticks
cookbook	**door**bell	**foot**ball	**foot**path
flowerpot	**grass**hopper	**horse**shoe	**ice** cream
milkman	**post** office	**milk** pot	**shoe** shop
suitcase	**sun**shade	**tea**cup	**tooth**paste

2 *Stress both the words in these noun phrases.*

first class	full moon	full-time	five-finger
hand-made	half-price	next door	North-East
twenty-five	three-wheeler	world-class	yellow butter

Compound nouns made up of two nouns usually have the main stress on the first part.

LEARN SOUNDS

Listen and repeat.

Stress in words made up of two syllables.

Words are made up of vowel and consonant sounds. Sometimes there is more than one vowel sound in a word. When this happens we need to pause slightly and take a short breath. We pronounce the words having one vowel sound at one go but break up words with more than one vowel sound into syllables. A syllable may contain only one vowel sound as in **a**/bout or a vowel and a consonant as in b**e**/g**i**n or as in **a**n/sw**e**r.

Nouns: stress on the first syllable	**ex**port	**con**tract **con**tent	**de**sert	**pre**sent	**pur**chase **pro**test	**re**cord	**ta**ble **to**wel
Verbs: stress on the second syllable	be**gin**	con**duct** con**tent**	ex**port**	pre**sent**	pro**test**	re**cord**	re**turn**
Adjectives: stress on the first syllable	**bum**py	**for**eign	**li**quid	**nas**ty	**se**rious	**to**tal	**truth**ful
Exceptions in verbs	**ans**wer	**pic**ture	**pro**mise	**sharp**en	**tra**vel	**vi**sit	
Exceptions in nouns	be**lief**	can**teen**	ca**nal**	ho**tel**	ma**chine**	pa**rade**	po**lice**

LISTEN AND LEARN

Listen to the following questions and their answers.

1. **A:** What did you do last evening?
   B: I watched a movie.
2. **A:** What did the children do in the summer vacation?
   B: They attended a theatre workshop.
3. **A:** When did the bell ring?
   B: About five minutes back.
4. **A:** Where did all the biscuits go?
   B: We ate them.
5. **A:** What happened to the milk?
   B: It turned sour.
6. **A:** How did the students travel?
   B: They travelled by the school bus.

SPEAK RIGHT

Listen and repeat. Listen to the questions and their answers. Then give answers of your own. Look at the bubbles for help.

1. Where did you pick this book?
2. How old was the young man in 2010?
3. Where did your friend live?
4. What jumped on the flower pot?
5. What did you buy?
6. At what price did you get this shirt?
7. Where are you off to?
8. Where's the photographer?

Begin with: At/About/To/In/For

a. the dark room

e. the post office

b. bookshop

f. some toothpaste and nail paint

c. a grasshopper

h. a hundred and fifty rupees

d. next door

g. twenty-seven

LISTEN AND SPEAK

Listen and repeat.

Short questions	What's your **name**? What's the **time**? Can you **sing**?
Commands	Cut it **open**. Shut the **door**. Put it **down**.

Other phrases	See you **later**. Thanks a **lot**. Yes, of **course**. Pleased to **meet** you. Nice to **see** you. Like to **eat** it? Take an **apple** first. Like to **buy** something? Wish to go **home**?

ROLE-PLAY

Work with a partner and play the roles of A and B. Read your role card and answer your partner's questions. Exchange roles.

A	B
Where did you go last summer?	We went to.......
When did you leave?	We went by/in a........
How did you go there?	We saw.......... (names of places, monuments, natural sights, markets, museums, etc.)
What places did you see?	
Did you eat any nice dish?	We ate......... (name of any particular dish) made of........
Did you take any pictures?	Yes, we did.
Did you have any adventure?	Once, we got lost/missed the train, etc.

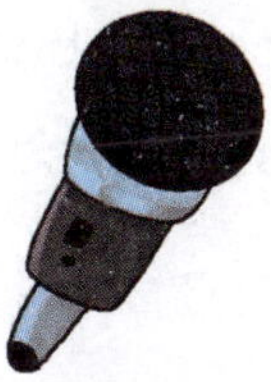

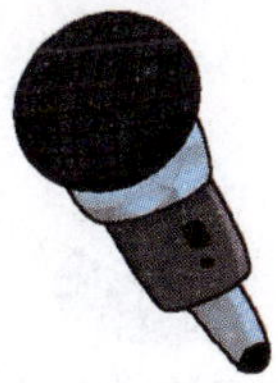

READ AND SPEAK

Talk about these actions in the past.

1. Preparations for the school Annual Day

clean	classroom, windows, blackboard
dust	desks, chairs, tables, shelves

decorate walls, door

yesterday, last week, last Saturday

2. A birthday party

have a party, a get together
eat cake, *vadas, pooris, chola*
drink juice, cold drinks
play games, dance, listen to music
last weekend, last month,
on Monday

3. Teacher's Day

wish/greet teacher (name)
give card, a book
have sweets, some games

4. Vacation

relax
visit places, friends, relatives
read comics, storybooks
watched television, movies

3 Making Offers

LISTEN AND LEARN

Little Lucy enters a magic door and reaches Rhyme Kingdom. Listen to her and understand how she offers help to different people there.

To make offers, say: **Shall I...? Can I...?**

To accept, say: **Yes, please./Thank you very much./Thanks very much.**

To refuse, say: **No, thank you. I'm fine./No, thank you./No, not now,** etc.

LISTEN AND REPEAT

Listen carefully and repeat the following contractions.

I'm
she's
he's
you're
we're
they're
they can't
she won't
she'll
he'll
let's
they'd
he'd
they'll
I'll
you'd
I'd
she'd

LISTEN AND CHOOSE

Listen and cross what you didn't hear in each response.

1. **A:** Why haven't you done the homework?
   B: But I have/I've.
2. **A:** She'll not come to the party.
   B: I know she will/she'll.
3. **A:** The train's running late.
   B: No, it's not/it isn't.
4. **A:** The sale's over, isn't it?
   B: No, it's not/it isn't.
5. **A:** You're angry, aren't you?
   B: Of course, I am/I'm.
6. **A:** I'm sure they'll have to wait.
   B: No, they will not/they'll not have to. All arrangements are done.
7. **A:** They're worried about their marks, I'm sure.
   B: No, they aren't/they're not. Look how they are/they're playing.
8. **A:** Why hasn't he answered my letter yet?
   B: But he has/he's.

LEARN SOUNDS

Listen and repeat.

1

-able		-al		-er/-or		-ful	
drink	**drink**able	ar**rive**	ar**riv**al	**act**	**act**or	**hand**	**hand**ful
read	**read**able	**mu**sic	**mu**sical	**read**	**read**er	**cheer**	**cheer**ful
wash	**wash**able	**cli**nic	**cli**nical	**walk**	**walk**er	**care**	**care**ful

-hood		-ment		-ness	
child	**child**hood	**move**	**move**ment	**hap**py	**hap**piness
boy	**boy**hood	**pay**	**pay**ment	**neat**	**neat**ness
neighbour	**neigh**bourhood	en**joy**	en**joy**ment	**dark**	**dark**ness

-ship		-ing		-ise/-ize	
friend	**friend**ship	**ask**	**ask**ing	**na**tional	**na**tionalise
citizen	**ci**tizenship	**burn**	**burn**ing	**stan**dard	**stan**dardise
member	**mem**bership	**hope**	**hop**ing	**mem**ory	**mem**orize

-less		-ish		-ly	
help	**help**less	**fe**ver	**fe**verish	**bad**	**bad**ly
aim	**aim**less	**black**	**black**ish	**friend**	**friend**ly
count	**count**less	**book**	**book**ish	**loud**	**loud**ly
care	**care**less	**dark**	**dark**ish	**sud**den	**sud**denly

When suffixes **-able**, **-al**, **-er/-or**, **-ful**, **-hood**, **-ment**, **-ness**, **-ship**, **-ing**, **-ise/-ize**, **-less**, **-ish**, **-ly** are added to words to change the meaning, there is **no shift** in the stress.

But when suffixes **-tion**, **-cian**, **-ic**, **-ical** are added, the stress shifts to the penultimate syllable, i.e the last but one syllable.

2

-tion		-cian	
add	**add**ition	clinic	cli**ni**cian
attend	at**ten**tion	**elec**tric	elec**tri**cian
celebrate	cele**bra**tion	**op**tic	op**ti**cian
collect	col**lec**tion	**ma**gic	ma**gi**cian
direct	di**rec**tion	mathe**ma**tics	mathema**ti**cian
educate	edu**ca**tion	**mu**sic	mu**si**cian

-ic		-ical	
artist	ar**tis**tic	**bo**tany	bo**ta**nical
atom	a**to**mic	**cone**	**co**nical
drama	dra**ma**tic	e**co**logy	eco**lo**gical
magnet	mag**ne**tic	**num**ber	nu**me**rical
majesty	ma**jes**tic	**gram**mar	gram**ma**tical
period	pe**rio**dic	**po**litic	po**li**tical

ROLE-PLAY

Speak with a partner.

1. **A:** Shall I carry your bag?
   B: No, thank you. I can manage.
2. **A:** Can I get you something to eat?
   B: That'd be lovely. I'm hungry.
3. **A:** Can I hold it for you?
   B: Thank you very much.
4. **A:** Shall I pay for you?
   B: Yes, please. I think I've left my purse at home.
5. **A:** Shall I colour the pictures for you?
   B: No, thank you. I'll colour them myself.
6. **A:** Can I help you?
   B: Yes. Please switch on the laptop for me.

LISTEN AND MARK

Listen and answer. Tick the correct box.

1. Where is EsselWorld situated?
   a. near Chennai ☐
   b. near Delhi ☐
   c. near Mumbai ☐
2. What does EsselWorld have?
   a. a water park ☐
   b. a theme park ☐
   c. a water park and a theme park ☐
3. Which was the scariest ride for Manasi?
   a. the roller coaster ☐
   b. Monsters in the Mist ☐
   c. the ride through water ☐
4. How can one reach the place easily?
   a. by taking a car and then a bus ride ☐
   b. by taking a train and then the ferry ☐
   c. by taking a direct bus from Mumbai ☐
5. Whose ticket is the cheapest?
   a. a child's ☐
   b. a grown up's ☐
   c. an older person's ☐
6. When are the tickets expensive?
   a. on holidays ☐
   b. on week days ☐
   c. on summer days ☐

SPEAK RIGHT

Listen and repeat.

1. a majestic mansion
2. boyhood friendship
3. a careful electrician
4. a friendly neighbourhood
5. a dramatic magician
6. a confident player
7. a botanical garden
8. a cheerful musician
9. a numerical problem
10. a readable book
11. an efficient clinician
12. a darkish washable fabric

READ AND SPEAK

Study the situation below and make offers to Rakesh.

Rakesh was going back home from the library. On the way, it started raining. A very strong wind began to blow. Rakesh struggled to hold his umbrella open. Suddenly, it flew off and fell a little away from him. While Rakesh was struggling with the umbrella, some of the books, which he was carrying in his hand, fell down in the puddle. Now, Rakesh is trying to hold on to the rest of the books and picking up the fallen ones. He is also getting wet in the rain.

Have you ever helped anyone out? How did you feel after helping the person? Do you think it's a good thing to help others? Tell the others in class.

Remember, you can use 'I think'/'I believe' to express your opinion on the matter.

4 Expressing Reason/Result

LISTEN AND LEARN

Mullah Nasruddin was known for his funny actions or remarks. Here are two funny incidents from his life. Notice how reasons are expressed.

One day, a neighbour went to borrow Mullah Nasruddin's donkey. Mullah did not wish to lend him his donkey because the man was not good at returning things he had borrowed.

As luck would have it, the donkey decided to bray right at that moment.

To give a reason for something, we use **because**.

I/She/He, etc. + (verb) + **because** + reason

To express the result of something, we use **so**. We first state the cause, then the result.

I can't find anything here. So I'll...(action)**.**

LISTEN AND MARK

Listen and circle the word you hear.

1. They add/added some more sugar.
2. I want/wanted to buy a camera.
3. We correct/corrected all the errors.
4. They waste/wasted a lot of time.
5. Atul and his mother wait/waited for the doctor.
6. These dresses suit/suited Malathi very well.
7. We note/noted whatever our teacher said.
8. We wade/waded through the puddles of water.

LISTEN AND LEARN

Listen and repeat.

1. She speaks English well.
2. He reads many books. He also watches English films.
3. He rushes out of his home at 7.00 every morning.
4. He never misses his classes. He always comes first.
5. George's mother is unwell. Ridge's mother watches over her.
6. Turn the pages fast.
7. Jess's brother broke his glasses.
8. We had three lunches at the new restaurant.
9. They sell purses and watches.
10. Tina misses her school bus every day.

LEARN SOUNDS

Listen and repeat these compound words.

Compound Nouns (stress on first word)	**cock**crow	**back**ground	**bath**room	**butter**fly	**chop**stick
	eggplant	**drain**pipe	**dust**pan	**ear**phone	**earth**quake
	sunflower	**fire**man	**foot**print	**grass**hopper	**key**hole
	armchair	**market**place	**note**book	**pass**word	**rain**bow
	clockwork				
	eyelid				
	ladybug				

Compound Adjectives (stress on both) Compound adjectives are made of two or more adjectives.	**full-length**	**good-looking**	**brightly-lit**
	last-minute	**English-speaking**	**pea-green**
	fast-moving	**pitch-dark**	**light-brown**
	well-known	**twenty-storey**	**well-behaved**
	sure-footed	**long-lasting**	**ready-made**

Compound Verbs (stress on the second word) Compound verbs are made of two or more verbs.	out**grow**	out**do**	over**hear**	fore**see**
	up**set**	under**take**	under**go**	way**lay**

Compound Adverbs (stress on both) Compound adverbs are made of two or more adverbs.	**everyday**	**everywhere**	**nowhere**
	therefore	**hereby**	**whereupon**
	somewhere		

LISTEN AND WRITE

Listen to a conversation and complete the information.

SPORTS CLUB

Name of the club ....

....

Student membership fee ....

....

Sibling concession ....

....

Distance from Colony A ....

....

Days .... to ....

Timings .... to ....

Sport well known for ....

....

....

LISTEN AND LEARN

Listen and repeat.

1. **A:** Why did you leave early yesterday?

   B: I left early because my grandparents were coming home.

2. **A:** Why don't you like toffees?

   B: I don't like toffees because they're sticky.

3. **A:** Why do you write notes on your palm?

   B: I write notes on my palm so that I can remember them easily.

4. **A:** Why didn't you come out to play?

   B: I had the project work to finish. So I didn't come out to play.

LISTEN AND MARK

You will hear some conversations. Listen and tick the correct answer.

1. Why did Rohini go to bed early?
   a. because she always does ☐
   b. because the next day was Sports Day ☐
   c. because she was tired ☐
2. Why didn't the nurse treat Atul?
   a. because it was not right for her to prescribe medicine ☐
   b. because the doctor was not in the clinic ☐
   c. because she didn't know much about stomach pain ☐
3. What did Atul and his mother decide to do?
   a. wait for the doctor to return ☐
   b. go home ☐
   c. take another appointment ☐

4. How will Lata celebrate her birthday?

   a. She will have a small party. ☐

   b. She will go to meet poor children. ☐

   c. She will take gifts for poor children. ☐

5. Why were Lata's parents happy to hear her decision?

   a. because they would not have to spend much ☐

   b. because she was going to do something different ☐

   c. because they believe in helping others ☐

ROLE-PLAY

Look at the two role cards and ask questions to your partner.

A

Find out reasons why:

1. Your friend was on leave for two days.
2. Your friend went home early.
3. Your friend is smiling secretly.
4. Your friend's mother has come to school.
5. Your friend does not like fairy tales.
6. Your friend is not going in the school bus.

B

Find out reasons why:

1. Your friend got late for school.
2. Your friend did not bring lunch to school.
3. Your friend is quiet in the class.
4. Your friend wants to meet the Principal.
5. Your friend does not like ghost stories.
6. Your friend's mother calls up during the lunch break.

5 Talking about Ongoing Actions in the Past

LISTEN AND LEARN

Granny made some cookies for the big weekend party and put them in two nice jars. But they disappeared. Listen how Inspector Findout interviews all the suspects in the case. Notice how actions of the past are talked about.

To talk about actions going on in the past, we use the past continuous tense of verbs.

I/He/She was + verb + **ing**....

You/We/They were +verb + **ing**....

To ask someone about actions going on in the past, we say:

What was+ he/she/(name) **do** + **ing**....?

What were you/they do + **ing**....?

Was it rain + **ing**?

LISTEN AND MATCH

You will hear some children talking about an earthquake that struck the previous night. What was each child doing at that time? Write a letter (A–E) next to each person.

A chatting in bed
B packing school bag
C having a little quarrel over a book
D helping father put away the dishes
E watching favourite cartoon

1. 
Tanya ☐

2. 
Rahul ☐

3. 
Bhola ☐

4. 
Hardeep ☐ **Jasmeet** ☐

5. 

Venkat ☐ **Malti** ☐

LISTEN AND MARK

Listen to the children talk about the things that happened on the day of the earthquake. If you can hear the /t/, /d/ or /id/ clearly at the end of the verb in the sentence, mark it with a tick.

1. Oh, the dish in my hand landed on the floor and broke.
2. I was very scared and shouted, "MUMMY!"
3. We stopped quarrelling and held each other tightly.
4. We jumped off the bed and ran outside.
5. Oh, I yelled. I wished the rumbling would stop.
6. I closed my books and sprinted towards the balcony.

LISTEN AND LEARN

Listen and repeat.

1. I have added two teaspoons of sugar in your milk.
2. Yesterday we potted some plants in the garden.
3. Have you washed your hands?
4. Mother picked me up from school today.
5. My friend Prasanna has moved out from this colony.
6. Our team bagged three prizes.
7. They loaded all their things onto a large truck.
8. We pushed the table to the corner to get some extra space.
9. Rupa liked the dress her aunt gave her.
10. Have you filled the buckets with water?

LISTEN AND WRITE

You will hear some information about Tiger Hill. Listen and fill in the missing details.

Tiger Hill

Location: At the .... of Ghum in ....

Distance from the town: ....

Ways to reach there: By jeep or ....

You can see: .... over the mountains

Name of the mountain range: ....

Most suitable time to see the sunrise: ....

SPEAK RIGHT

Say the sentences given below.

1. I wasn't riding my bicycle. I was reading my book.
2. I was feeling nervous. So I filled in only a part of the form.
3. Father was grating carrots while Mother was grading assignments.
4. We were waiting for the loaded truck. Soon it rolled heavily up the road.
5. The patient was groaning and moaning in the morning.
6. We raised an alarm and chased the thief.

LEARN SOUNDS

Listen and repeat.

Verb	Past Tense 'ed' as /t/	Verb	Past Tense 'ed' as /d/	Verb	Past Tense 'ed' as a separate syllable /Id/
tap	tapped	rob	robbed	add	added
lick	licked	beg	begged	wait	waited
miss	missed	buzz	buzzed	pat	patted
laugh	laughed	move	moved	need	needed
munch	munched	budge	budged	lift	lifted
push	pushed	measure	measured	nod	nodded
wrap	wrapped	store	stored	note	noted

SPEAK AND WRITE

Say the words aloud and put them in the right columns in the table given on the next page. Compare your table with your partner's.

cheered bowled looked billed stuffed boarded
created packed rested pressed lived floated

'ed' sounds like /t/	'ed' sounds like /d/	'ed' sounds like /ɪd/

LISTEN, READ AND SPEAK

Listen to the description of this pretty toy train that runs in the Himalayan mountains. Tick the statements as correct (✓) or incorrect (✗). Say the correct sentences aloud. Take turns with your partner.

Toy Train of Darjeeling Himalayan Railway

1. The Darjeeling Himalayan Railway is also called the 'Baby Train'.
2. It has normal railway tracks.
3. It runs between Siliguri and Darjeeling in West Bengal.
4. The railway was built more than a hundred years ago.
5. It starts at New Jalpaiguri and ends its journey at Kurseong.
6. The toy train from Darjeeling to Ghum is pulled by modern locomotives.
7. The Darjeeling Himalayan Railway has still not been declared a World Heritage Site.

Listen carefully to the audio once again, correct the sentences and say the incorrect sentences correctly.

ROLE-PLAY

Talk to five students in your class and find out what each was doing at these times on last Sunday.

1. 7 a.m. 2. 11 a.m. 3. 1 p.m. 4. 5 p.m. 5. 8 p.m. 6. 10 p.m.

You may use sentences like: *What were you doing around 7 a.m./7 in the morning?*

Record your findings and report them to the class. You may use sentences like these:

At 7 a.m., three of them were still in bed.

At 5 p.m., two were out shopping with their parents. Two were completing the English homework and one was chatting with his friend.

6 Expressing Possibility

LISTEN AND LEARN

Little Papiya went to a fair and got lost there. Her family is looking for her. Listen to people expressing different possibilities.

To express possibility (may be true or may/may not happen), we use **may**.

I may go out today. **She may be in the library.**

To express that something is not possible, we use **may not**.

We may not go for the picnic.

LISTEN AND MARK

Answer the questions by encircling the correct option.

1. Which city is Hiranyamoy from?

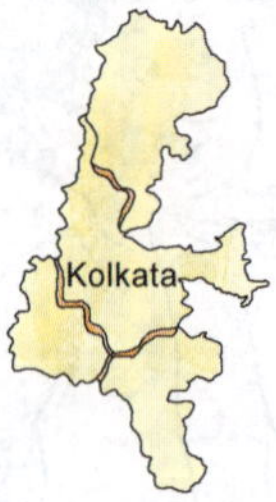

A

B

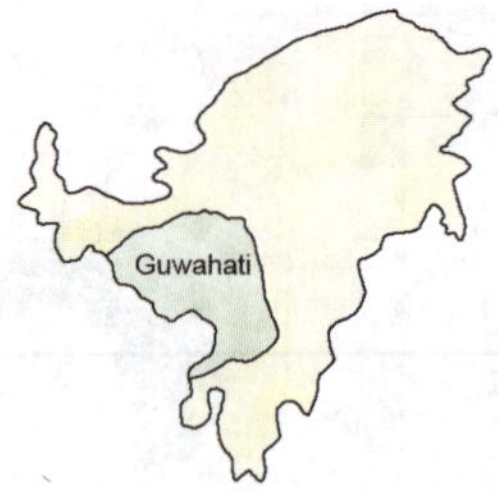

C

2. What did Madhu find amazing in France?

Cruise

A

Eiffel Tower

B

Louvre

C

3. When will the solar eclipse begin?

A

B

C

4. What kind of weather will Isabel find in Srinagar?

A

B

C

5. How far is Cherrapunjee from Shillong?

A

B

C

LISTEN AND WRITE

Look at the pictures. Listen and complete the sentences.

1.

A: Would you like to try this new fruit?

B: I'm not too sure. It .... be sour.

Why have the cow and the calf come here?

A: They .... have come here for shade.

B: They .... have come here for food as well.

Or, perhaps, they .... be looking for their master.

2.

LISTEN AND LEARN

Listen and repeat.

1. Tomorrow is a holiday. I may go to my grandfather's house.
2. Let's fill these coupons in. We may be lucky to win free tickets.
3. There are dark clouds in the sky. It may rain.
4. Listen to his accent. He may be English.
5. She may not answer my call. She may have slept already.
6. I may be on the wrong bus. Let me ask someone.
7. Don't worry about the test. It may not be so difficult.

LEARN SOUNDS

Listen carefully. Pay attention to how the words in bold are said. Repeat. Notice how we raise our voice when the arrows point upwards and lower it when the arrows point downwards. These are rising intonation and falling intonation.

1. **A:** Weren't you ↗ **sleeping** when the phone rang?

   B: Well, I was not ↘ **sleeping**. I was ↘ **reading** in bed.

2. **A:** I thought the ↗ **ice cream** was very good.

   B: I thought the ↘ **pudding** was ↗ **better**.

3. **A:** Is that a ↗ **deer** under the tree?

   B: No, that's not a ↘ **deer**. That's a large ↘ **goat**.

4. **A:** Where are these bells from?

   B: They are from ↘ **Philadelphia**.

5. **A:** Wasn't it ↗ **Rohan** who won the first prize?

   B: Well, it wasn't ↘ **Rohan**. It was his ↘ **brother**.

LISTEN AND MARK

Listen and mark the intonation of the words in bold with ↗ or ↘.

1. **A:** Do you want to go to the supermarket on **Saturday** or **Sunday**?

   B: We'll go on **Sunday.**

2. **A:** Is your birthday in **March** or **April**?

   B: It's in **March.**

3. **A:** What would you like-**coffee**, **tea** or **juice**?

   B: I'll have some **juice.**

4. **A:** Shall we watch a **cartoon** or the **quiz**?

   B: Let's watch the **quiz.**

5. **A:** Would you like to have **Indian** or **Chinese food**?

   B: **Chinese**, please.

6. **A:** Did she go to **Italy** or **France** last year?

   B: She went to **Italy**.

LOOK AND SPEAK

Look at the pictures. What may happen if you ignore these warnings?

Answer using words from the box. Say a sentence or two about each. The first one has been done for you.

dog bite
jump on
growl at

The dog may bite you.
The dog may jump on you.

bees
sting
attack

police
catch
fine

things
fall on
head

you get
shock
burn

you slip
fall down

SPEAK RIGHT

Say the sentences using the rising intonation for the words in bold. Work with a partner.

1. **A:** Let's go to Shimla. It is a nice place.

   B: But Mussoorie is **nicer**.

2. **A:** Look, this shirt is good.

   B: I know it's good but the other one is **better**.

3. **A:** Her bag is pretty.

   B: I know but yours is **prettier**.

4. **A:** Going by bus is cheap.

   B: But the train is **cheaper**.

5. **A:** Eating eggs is healthy.

   B: No, I think eating fish is **healthier**.

6. **A:** I think the movie was good.

   B: I think the book is **better**.

ROLE-PLAY

Talk to your partner and ask him/her to tell you about things he/she is likely to do in the next one year. Use may in your answers.

1. Tell me a place you are likely to go to in the summer.
2. What is it that you may buy in the next one year?
3. Do you plan to do anything special in the next one year?
4. Which storybooks do you plan to read in the next year?
5. Do you plan to learn anything new in the next one year?
6. What are your plans for the coming Sunday?

7 Talking about Actions in Relation to Other Actions

LISTEN AND LEARN

Listen to the story of the blue jackal and notice how one action is discussed in relation to thc othcr.

A clever jackal from the jungle went to the village to steal some hens. The hens belonged to the village washerman. There, he fell into a tub of blue colour that the washerman used to dye clothes.

The village dogs saw the jackal and chased him away.

The clever jackal came up with a cunning plan.
I'm Royal Blue, a messenger of the gods. I have come to rule and protect all of you. You must obey me.
I have never seen an animal like him. He is not an ordinary animal like us. I'm sure he is very powerful. Let's do what he says before he gets angry and punishes us.
Hmpf, I agree.

So, the jackal enjoyed his time in the jungle and all the animals obeyed him.
Tell me the names of the wicked animals before we begin our daily round of the forest.
O, Royal Blue, all animals have become good after you came here. They follow your laws.

One night, all the jackals in the jungle started to howl. Now, it's the habit of jackals that when one of them howls, the others also feel like howling. The clever jackal forgot that he was playing the part of 'Royal Blue' and started to howl too!

After that night, the cunning jackal did not go back to the jungle.

To talk about the sequence of two actions that happened at two different times, we use **before** or **after**. To indicate that one happened earlier, we use **before**. To indicate that one happened later, we use **after**.

LISTEN AND MATCH

Listen and match the items in the two columns. Write the correct letter in the box. What did the children ask for at the cafe?

1. Ranbir ☐ — A. 

2. Mitali ☐ — B. 

3. Rita ☐ — C. 

4. Sudeep ☐ — D. 

5. Gagan ☐ — E. 

6. Rana ☐ — F. 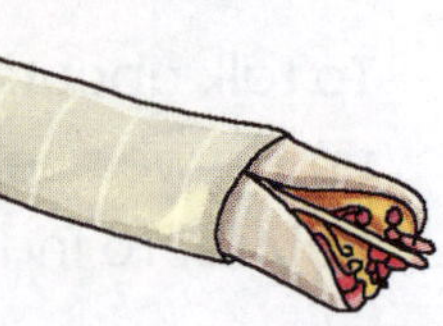

LISTEN AND WRITE

You will hear a conversation between Raman and his neighbour about a sightseeing trip. Listen carefully and complete the information given below.

Sightseeing Trip in New Delhi

1. Places visited before lunch:

   a. First, ... at 10 in ....

   b. Then, the Safdarjung Tomb at about ....

2. Lunch break at 2 p.m. in the ....

3. Places visited after lunch:

   a. .... before going into the ....

   b. the cinema

4. Coffee break at .... in the ....

LISTEN AND LEARN

Listen and repeat. Note the different intonations in the first and the second half of the sentences.

1. I was coming down the ↗ **stairs** last evening, and I found a ↘ **ring** on the last ↘ **step**.
2. I was looking for ↗ **mother** in the garden, and I saw this ↘ **monkey**.
3. I was reading the ↗ **newspaper** one morning, and I came upon this ↘ **funny** advertisement.
4. They were ready to go to ↗ **bed**, when they heard this strange ↘ **sound** coming from the ↘ **wardrobe**.
5. She was watching ↗ **TV** one evening, and she saw her ↘ **friend** participating in a dance ↘ **show**.

Rising intonation

a. ↗ **stairs** last evening—down the ↗ **stairs** last evening—I was coming down the ↗ **stairs** last evening.

b. ↗ **bicycle** in the lane—riding my ↗ **bicycle** in the lane—She was riding her ↗ **bicycle** in the lane.

c. ↗ **song** for the show—rehearsing our ↗ **song** for the show—We were rehearsing our ↗ **song** for the show.

Falling intonation

a. a ↘ **ring**—a ↘ **ring** on the last ↘ **step**—and I saw a ↘ **ring** on the last ↘ **step**

b. this ↘ **kitten**—this ↘ **kitten** under a ↘ **lamp** post—and she saw this↘ **kitten** under the ↘ **lamp** post

c. a ↘ **shriek**—a ↘ **shriek** in the next ↘ **house**—and we heard a ↘ **shriek** in the next ↘ **house**

LISTEN AND LEARN

Listen and repeat. Remember to raise your voice at the upward arrow and lower it at the downward arrow.

Kaamini was walking ↗ **home** from school one day as ↗ **usual**, and she found a baby ↘ **bird** under a ↘ **bush**. She stood there ↗ **looking** at the bird thinking that it would ↘ **die**, if it ↘ **lay** there on the ↘ **ground** for long. She ↗ **picked** it up and looked ↗ **around** for its ↘ **nest**. A few moments ↗ **later** she heard some excited ↘ **chirping**. She now knew where the ↗ **nest** was and put the ↗ **baby** in it.

A couple of weeks ↗ **later**, Kaamini was pleased to find the ↗ **baby**, now all ↗ **grown** up, hopping in the ↘ **bushes** with its ↘ **parents**.

LISTEN AND LEARN

Listen carefully.

as ↗ **usual** and ↗ **suddenly** under the ↘ **table** ↗ **picked** it up ↗ **around** for its ↘ **nest**

LISTEN AND SPEAK

Listen and retell the story. Remember to raise your voice at the upward arrow and lower it at the downward arrow.

Piyush was practising ↗ **music** one day as ↗ **usual**, when he heard a ↘ **shriek** from under the ↘ **table**. He stood up ↗ **looking** for the source of the ↗ **shriek** and saw this tiny ↘ **man** on the ↘ **floor**. So he bent ↗ **down** and picked him ↗ **up** and asked him his ↘ **name** but the man went on ↘ **shrieking**. "This music of ↗ **yours** is too bad for my ↘ **taste**," he ↘ **said**. A couple of weeks ↗ **later**, Piyush was sitting and ↗ **drawing**, and he saw the little man ↘ **again**. "You draw ↗ **better** than you ↘ **sing**," he said. Piyush put him on the ↗ **table** and ↘ **smiled** at ↗ **him** and ↗ **suddenly** he thought, "I ↘ **know** ↗ **him.**" The man had the ↘ **face** of a ↘ **famous** musician.

ROLE-PLAY

Speak with a partner.

1. **A:** What time did you leave school?

   B: I think I left before you did.

   A: No, it can't be. I left immediately after the bell.

   B: Then you're right. I met the head teacher after school. I left only after I spoke to her.

2. **A:** Excuse me, I was here before you. Can I buy my ticket first?

   B: No, I don't think so. You came after I did.

   A: Well, what time did you come to the booth?

   B: Um...mmm a little after eleven, I guess.

   A: I have been in the queue since half past ten. That means I was here before you. Now please let me buy my tickets.

3. **A:** I always brush my teeth after I get up in the morning.

   B: Don't you brush your teeth before going to bed?

   A: No, is that necessary?

   B: Well, my dentist has asked me to brush my teeth soon after waking up and before going to bed every day.

4. **A:** What time is it?

   B: I think it is six.

   A: No, it can't be. The sun is still over the trees.

8 Expressing Conditions

LISTEN AND LEARN

Listen to the instructions being given to the students at a camp and notice how conditions are expressed.

To state a condition, we use **If**.

If + subject + verb in the simple present...

If you wear a cap on chilly mornings, you will feel comfortable.

LISTEN AND CHOOSE

Listen to the conversations and match the conditions with their result. Tick the right box.

1. If you receive a gift in England, you must say "Thank you" and
   a. politely keep it aside. ☐
   b. put it in your bag. ☐
   c. open it in front of others. ☐

2. If you are eating in Indonesia, you must never
   a. stand and eat while at home. ☐
   b. stand and eat while in a restaurant. ☐
   c. stand or walk while eating anywhere. ☐

3. If you are invited to a traditional Indian home, you should always
   a. wear chappals to the host's house. ☐
   b. take off your footwear before entering the house. ☐
   c. enter properly dressed with your footwear on. ☐

4. If you buy two shirts at 'Sharp Apparels', you will
   a. get a third one free. ☐
   b. get a discount of 10%. ☐
   c. get a handkerchief free. ☐

5. If you pay your membership at the Culture Club for three years at once, you will
   a. not have to pay any more. ☐
   b. get to see extra movies. ☐
   c. get a discount on the membership. ☐

LISTEN AND LEARN

Listen and repeat.

1. **A:** Would you know when the next train will ↗ **arrive**?

   B: ↗ **Sorry?**

2. **A:** You know it rained heavily last ↗ **night**?

   B: Did ↗ **it?** I didn't hear ↘ **anything**.

3. **A:** We were waiting for an ↗ **autorickshaw**, and it ↗ **suddenly** began to ↘ **rain**.

   B: Did ↗ **it?** What did you ↘ **do**?

   A: Well, we ran for shelter and found ↗ **none** nearby.

   B: That's ↘ **terrible**.

4. **A:** They announced something ↗ **interesting** at the assembly ↘ **today**.

   B: ↗ **Really?** ↗ **What** was ↘ **it**?

   A: They're building a swimming pool in the ↘ **school**.

   B: That's ↗ **great!**

5. **A:** It's rather ↗ **windy** today.

   B: What did you ↗ **say**?

   A: I said it's very ↘ **windy**. Please close the ↘ **window**.

   B: Oh, the ↗ **window**. Sure.

   A: ↘ **Thank** you.

One of the ways in which you can be a good listener is by asking questions to the speaker as done in the conversations above. This will help you to get the information you need.

LISTEN AND MARK

Listen and mark the correct answer to the questions.

1. What is the new phone called?
   a. a widget ☐
   b. a smart phone ☐
   c. a clever phone ☐

2. How can you dial a number on the phone?
   a. by pressing the buttons on the keyboard ☐
   b. by typing the numbers using a separate keyboard ☐
   c. by tapping the virtual keypad on the touch screen ☐

3. How can you make the numbers larger and easier to tap?
   a. by tilting the phone ☐
   b. by pressing a button ☐
   c. by tapping an icon ☐

4. What does the weather-widget show?
   a. weather for the hour ☐
   b. weather for the hour and day ☐
   c. weather for the hour, day and week ☐

5. What can one download for free on the phone that Rajni's mother's got?
   a. games ☐
   b. books and music ☐
   c. music, games and books ☐

LISTEN, READ AND SPEAK

Listen, read and complete the conversations.

Listen to the dialogues and choose the right response from the bubble. Say it aloud. Then play the roles with your friend.

Excellent!/That's good.
How nice!
When/Where/Why?
Did you?
Oh, no.
And then what happened?

1. **A:** I am leaving for Dehradun.

   B: .... ?

   A: On Sunday.

2. **A:** We have decided to go on a holiday.

   B: .... ?

   A: To Kerala.

   B: ....

3. **A:** We've finished all the work before time.

   B: ....

4. **A:** I may have to miss your party on Sunday.

   B: .... We were looking forward to seeing you.

5. **A:** Guess what! I rode to the city all alone on my bicycle.

   B: .... ? I hope you didn't have any problem on the way.

   A: I did. I lost my way. I kept riding within the lanes of the next colony and couldn't find the main road.

   B: .... ?

ROLE-PLAY

Imagine your partner is a person from Europe. You want to tell him/her about our culture. Provide information that will help him/her to be accepted by the local people. Think of creative ways of doing it.

1. **A:** I am planning to go visiting some local places this afternoon. Tell me a few things I should bear in mind.

   B: If someone greets you with a 'namaskar', you should try to do the same by putting your palms together. If someone helps you with directions to go somewhere, you should check the information out by asking a few more people.

2. **A:** I have heard about this good restaurant that serves South Indian food. I don't really know what to order. Do you have any suggestions?

   B: Hmm...if you go to a South Indian restaurant, you should ....

   ....

3. **A:** How does one greet people in India? Tell me a few polite ways of greeting.

   B: 'Namaskar' is a common greeting. If you see any lady, you can add 'Auntie' or 'Ma'am' to the 'namaskar'. If you see a person of your age

   ....

4. **A:** Hey, what does one do in the market? They say that if people see a foreigner they overcharge.

   B: If you keep shaking your head left and right to indicate 'no' then

   they may ....

5. **A:** I've been invited to a concert in Indian classical music. Have you any suggestions?

   B: If you go to a concert in Indian classical music, ...

   ....

9 Making Suggestions

LISTEN AND LEARN

Listen to the story of an emperor and notice how suggestions are made.

The emperor is coming. Let's pretend to be stitching a dress.
I can't see any cloth, tailors.
This is the best cloth in the kingdom. Only a fool will not be able to see it. Look carefully, your majesty.
Yes, yes. It's lovely, isn't it? How about having a parade to show my new dress!

Let's go to the front. They say that the emperor has new clothes on.
Sure, hold my hand.
Sh...let's pretend we can see them.
I don't see any new clothes, mother. In fact, the king has no clothes on!
No, I will not. Look! The emperor has no clothes on. The emperor has no clothes!

In order to make suggestions, we say:

Let's + verb...

Let's stop at the public library on the way home.

In order to suggest something in the form of a question, we say:

How about verb + **ing**....?

How about putting up pictures of your lost dog in the market?

LISTEN AND WRITE

Listen to a man asking for information about a sports academy and fill in the details.

State Sports Academy

1. Name of the sport: ....
2. Annual membership fee: ....
3. Days of tennis training: ....
4. Number of trainees per batch: ....
5. Name of the school: ....

LISTEN AND LEARN

Listen and repeat. Notice the stress on the words in bold.

1. **A:** How about **walking** to school today?
   B: Let's do that. It'd be nice for a change.
2. **A:** Let's **switch off** the AC and save some electricity.
   B: All right.
3. **A:** How about putting on a **play** on Teachers' Day?
   B: That's a good idea.
4. **A:** How about having a **quiz** today?
   B: Yes, that'd be wonderful.
5. **A:** Let's contribute this month's pocket money for the **flood victims**.
   B: That's a kind thought.

LISTEN AND LEARN

Listen and repeat. Remember to stress the words in bold.

1. **A:** How was the exhibition?

   B: The **science** one was good but the **history** one was boring.

2. **A:** I'll bring back a good collection of leaves from the hills.

   B: I'm not interested in **leaves.** Bring me some good **photographs**.

3. **A:** Can music help me concentrate?

   B: Only if you play it at a **low volume**.

4. **A:** Your mother writes Dr before her name. Is she a doctor?

   B: No, she is not a **doctor**. She's a **scientist**.

5. **A:** Can you cook well?

   B: Well, I can **cook** well, but I can't **bake** anything.

6. **A:** Is your school St Anthony?

   B: It's not **St Anthony** but **Frank Anthony**.

LISTEN AND MARK

Listen to the sentences and underline the stressed words. The first one has been done as an example.

1. **A:** How was the picnic?

   B: I enjoyed it a lot, but the bus journey was terrible.

2. **A:** When I grow up, I want to study maths.

   B: I hate maths, but I like science.

3. **A:** Are these apples from Himachal?

   B: No, not from Himachal, they're from Kashmir.

4. **A:** Do you have the details of the programme?

   B: I know it's this Saturday, but I don't know what time.

5. **A:** How was the match?

   B: Our bowling was pretty good, but our batting was terrible.

LISTEN AND CHOOSE

What did each person suggest about the old books at home?

Listen and write the correct letter in the box.

1. Mr Mehra ☐
2. Mrs Mehra ☐
3. Gagan ☐
4. Ishita ☐

A

B

C

D

E

F

SPEAK RIGHT

Say these sentences. Work in pairs.

1. **A:** Can I return the book to you on ↗ **Friday**?
   B: I won't be coming on ↘ **Friday**. I'll come on ↘ **Saturday** though.
2. **A:** Is your house number ↗ **L 12**?
   B: No, it is the ↘ **next** one. It's ↗ **L 12 A**.
3. **A:** Do you wear ↗ **long skirts**?
   B: I don't wear ↗ **long skirts**, but I ↘ **like** them.
4. **A:** What do you think of this ↗ **shirt**?
   B: I like the ↗ **colour**, but I feel it's a bit ↘ **short**.
5. **A:** I heard there are a hundred students in your ↘ **class**.
   B: Well, ↗ **nearly** ninety, I ↘ **think**.
6. **A:** How many times have you been to Delhi?
   B: I've ↘ **never** been to Delhi.

ROLE-PLAY

Agree or disagree with the given suggestions. You can use the words in bubbles for help. Work with a partner.

1. How about chatting on the Internet tonight?
2. Let's get Mahima the latest Harry Potter book.
3. How about a swim in the pool?
4. How about a running race?
5. How about going down to the cafeteria?

Sure.

Let's.

That's a good idea.

No, not now.

No, I don't feel like it.

Sorry, I am busy.

LISTEN AND LEARN

Listen to how Priya anchors the event of welcoming two new students to their class. Work in groups of six and take turns to anchor the farewell event for your favourite teacher, who is leaving for another city. Use the ideas given below.

1. Greet the class and the teacher. Introduce yourself and announce why they have assembled there.
2. Request the class monitor to say a few words about the teacher and to tell her how much everyone will miss him/her.
3. Request one more classmate to talk about the teacher and say how and why everyone liked him/her.
4. Thank your classmates for speaking. Request another classmate to give the teacher her farewell card/gift.
5. Now request the teacher to say a few words of encouragement and advice to the class.

LOOK, READ AND SPEAK

Look at the situations given below. Make as many suggestions as you can. Work in groups of six.

Use sentences like: *How about* ....

Let's ....

1. You find this cute dog wandering aimlessly on the roadside. You feel the dog is lost. It might also be hungry. You want to help.

2. Your cousin from Canada is visiting India for the first time. She will be landing in the hot month of May. You want her to pack wisely.

10 Expressing Obligation

LISTEN AND LEARN

Listen how Tutul's mother tells her to be careful while she is alone at home and notice how obligations are expressed.

To express obligation, we use **must/must not**.

You must not give any butter to the baby.

You must wear your school uniform every day to school.

LISTEN AND MARK

You will hear a conversation between a dentist and a boy, Sam, about how to take care of the new braces he has on his teeth.

Decide if each sentence is correct or not. If it is correct, choose the letter A. If it is not correct then choose B.

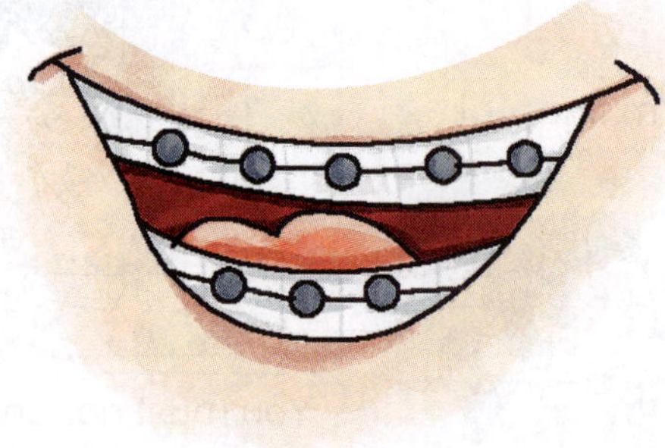

1.	Sam must not eat nuts, chewing gum or popcorn.	**A**	**B**
2.	Sam must use a hard toothbrush to clean the brackets well.	**A**	**B**
3.	Sam must not use dental floss while he has the braces.	**A**	**B**
4.	Sam must use dental wax between the bracket and the inside of his cheek.	**A**	**B**
5.	Sam must not take out the wax every time he brushes his teeth.	**A**	**B**
6.	Sam must rinse his mouth with warm salt water in the first week.	**A**	**B**

LISTEN AND LEARN

Listen and repeat.

1. It's 10 o'clock. You must go to bed now.
2. You mustn't scratch the wound. It may bleed again.
3. You mustn't leave anything on the plate. It is not good to waste food.

4. Come with me. You must not cross the road alone.
5. We must call her up tomorrow. She will worry if you don't.
6. There has been a burglary in their house. They must report it to the police.
7. I feel guilty. I must not hide anything from my mother.
8. She must not ride her bicycle so fast. She may have a fall.

LISTEN AND LEARN

Listen and repeat carefully.

1. **A:** I hope your report will be ready by ↘ **tomorrow**?

   B: ↗ **Tomorrow**? You can have it in an ↘ **hour**.

2. **A:** Is that your ↘ **assignment**?

   B: ↗ **That?** You must be ↘ **joking**.

3. **A:** Have you finished ↘ **dinner**?

   B: ↗ **Finished!** I've just ↘ **started** it.

4. **A:** You're ↘ **cheating**! You said ↘ **thirty rupees**!

   B: I ↘ **didn't!** I said ↘ **thirty-five**.

5. **A:** You can sing very well, ↘ **can't you**?

   B: ↗ **Me?** I've never sung in my ↘ **life.**

6. **A:** Are those your ↘ **books**?

   B: ↗ **Those?** No, those are ↘ **Aruna's**.

LISTEN AND MARK

Listen to the dialogues and mark the main words that are said with emphasis.

1. **A:** How was the movie?

   B: The first half was quite good. The second half was boring.

2. **A:** Did you have dinner at Mocambo last night?

   B: No, not at Mocambo. We ate at Thali.

3. **A:** How do you like the plums?
   B: The dark ones are fine. The light ones are sour.
4. **A:** How was your journey to Imphal?
   B: The onward journey was comfortable. The return journey was a bit difficult.
5. **A:** How do you like the house?
   B: The front is all right. The backyard is a bit shabby.

LISTEN AND WRITE

You will hear a description of a building. Listen carefully and complete the information.

1. Actually a .... which looks like a huge ....
2. Serves as the .... of the Longaberger Company
3. Situated in: Ohio, ...
4. Was built in ....
5. Number of storeys ....
6. Size: .... times that of a medium-sized basket
7. Basic shape: narrow at the bottom and .... at the top
8. Looks more beautiful at ....

World's Largest Basket

Did you come across any new words in the piece that you listened to? List them down. In pairs, talk to your partner about what you think the words mean. Look up a dictionary to see if you are correct.

SPEAK RIGHT

Listen and repeat. Remember to stress the words in bold.

1. **A:** Do you like ↘ papaya?
   B: ↗ **Me**? I ↘ **hate** it.
2. **A:** Was the train ↘ crowded?
   B: ↗ **Crowded**? It was ↘ **packed** to the last inch.
3. **A:** Is she good at ↘ singing?
   B: ↗ **She**? Not at all.
4. **A:** Are the tomatoes ↘ fresh?
   B: ↗ **Fresh**? They couldn't be ↘ **fresher**.
5. **A:** Did it rain ↘ **well**?
   B: ↗ **Rained**? It simply ↘ **poured**.
6. **A:** Is the patient ↘ walking?
   B: ↗ **Walking**? He's ↘ **running**.
7. **A:** Would you like to eat ↘ now?
   B: ↗ **Now?** It's much too ↘ **early** for dinner.
8. **A:** Do you like ↘ **pineapples**?
   B: ↗ **Like**? I simply ↘ love them.

READ AND WRITE

Read the phrases and write a sentence using 'must' or 'must not' for the given situations. Use the clues given below. You may use your own ideas too.

a. look left and right
b. wash them before eating/not eat before washing
c. keep quiet/not talk loudly
d. see the doctor/not go to school
e. be quiet/not shout
f. be careful/not break
g. follow the rules/not make noise
h. go to bed/not stay up any longer
i. answer it/not take long to reply
j. hurry up

1. The vase is made of glass. You

2. Aarti is ill. She

3. You have only ten minutes left to complete your test. You

4. Unwashed fruit and vegetables may have germs.

   We

5. People go to the library to study quietly. You

6. Running across a road can be dangerous. You

7. The baby is asleep. You ....

....

....

8. You look very tired. You ....

....

....

9. Rudra has written a lovely letter. I ....

....

....

10. This is a library. You ....

....

....

....

Read Aloud

PASSAGE 1: Tina Auntie's New Menu

First, listen to this story. Follow the story in your book. Then read aloud the story. Remember to give an extra emphasis to the words in bold. Also, pause where you find stroke marks (/). Stop at the end of sentences.

Everyone was **gathering** around the **canteen./Students** were **taking** a very **long time/**to **decide what** to **eat./Tina Auntie stood** at the **counter,/patiently waiting** for the **students/**to **make** up their **minds./**They **seemed** to be very **confused./**

The **reason** for this **confusion/**was that the **menu/**had been **changed** over the **weekend./**

Earlier,/the **menu** had **burgers,/fries,/cookies/**and **cold drinks./Today,/**the **burgers** were **gone/**and **so** were the **fries./**The **sweet buns** had **disappeared./Even** cold **drinks** had been **replaced/**by **fresh fruits** and **lemonade./**In **place** of **chocolate cookies,/millet cookies** had **appeared./**

"**Auntie,/**what are **millet cookies**?"**/**asked **Mita,/**a **Class 4 student./**

"**Millet cookies** are made of jowar, bajra and ragi.**/**They're **healthier,"/Auntie explained./**

"**Where** are the **samosas,/Auntie**?"**/Puran,/Mita's classmate,/entered** the **canteen/ nearly** out of **breath./**He had been **running all** the **way/**to the **canteen/holding** his **precious fifty rupee note./**

"**Sorry, Puran./**No **samosas today./**Why don't you have **poha**?"**/**asked **Tina Auntie./**

"**Poha,/where**?"**/**asked **Baljeet./He** had **run/**or almost **slid** into the **canteen** at **Puran's heels./**

"**There,/" Auntie pointed** to a **covered glass bowl/**with something that **looked** more like **porridge./**

"It **looks** so **colourful,"/said Mita./**

"**Indeed,/**it **does./This** is **because/**it has **lots** of **seasonal vegetables** in it,"**/Tina Auntie explained./**"**Hurry** up.**/Make up** your **minds fast/**or the **recess** will be **over**,"**/** she **cautioned./**

"**Ok/**. I shall have the **samosa/**,...no**/**...poha,**/**I **mean**,"**/**said **Puran** in a **small voice./**

"How about **trying** the **millet cookies,/Simran**?"**/Mita** said to her **friend./**

"**Sure,/they look** like they are **going** to be **tasty**,"**/Simran** said **enthusiastically./**

In **this way/Tina Auntie's Millet Savvy Canteen/slowly began** to **buzz** with **activity,/** the **usual chatter** of the **children/**and the **clinking** of **cutlery./**

POEM 1: Where Go the Boats?

Listen to the poem. Then read it aloud.

Dark brown is the river.
Golden is the sand.
It flows along for ever,
With trees on either hand.
Green leaves a-floating,
Castles of the foam,
Boats of mine a-boating—
Where will all come home?
On goes the river
And out past the mill,
Away down the valley,
Away down the hill.
Away down the river,
A hundred miles or more,
Other little children
Shall bring my boats ashore.

Robert Louis Stevenson

POEM 2: What Is Pink?

Listen to the poem. Then read it aloud.

What is pink? a rose is pink
By a fountain's brink.
What is red? a poppy's red
In its barley bed.
What is blue? the sky is blue
Where the clouds float thro'.
What is white? a swan is white
Sailing in the light.
What is yellow? pears are yellow,
Rich and ripe and mellow.
What is green? the grass is green,
With small flowers between.
What is violet? clouds are violet
In the summer twilight.
What is orange? why, an orange,
Just an orange!

Christina Rossetti

Revision Videos

Short Vowels

Long Vowels

Diphthongs

Consonants

Short vowel sounds as in	bat, sell, pin, ten, stop, nest, bus, gas, fill, fan, fun, again
Long vowel sounds as in	feet, seat, meet, beach, cute, food, soon, bird, curd, art, calm, talk, call
Dipthongs as in	name, cake, bone, rope, kite, light, coil, boil, loud, clown, here, dear, there, pair, poor, tour
Consonant sounds as in	pet, top, bat, deep, cat, goat, five, the, wash, measure, size, change, wind, always, vase, advise, think, teeth, yell, hero